CW01497189

THE SLIPPING FORECAST

First published in 2025 by
The Dedalus Press
13 Moyclare Road
Baldoyle
Dublin D13 K1C2
Ireland

www.dedaluspress.com

ISBN 9781915629357 (paperback)
ISBN 9781915629340 (hardback)

Dedalus Press titles are available in Ireland
from Argosy Books (www.argosybooks.ie) and in the UK
from Inpress Books (www.inpressbooks.co.uk).
Printed in Ireland by Print Dynamics.

Cover painting *Head Study 3* (21x14cm)
Gouache on Paper, by Craig Jefferson,
by kind permission.
www.craigjefferson.com

Dedalus Press receives financial assistance from
The Arts Council / An Chomhairle Ealaíon.

THE SLIPPING FORECAST

ROSS THOMPSON

DEDALUS PRESS

ACKNOWLEDGEMENTS

The author wishes to thank the publishers and editors of the following where a number of these poems, or versions of them, originally appeared:

Apricot Press, The Arts Show, Atrium, The Bangor Literary Journal, Dear Reader, the Dedalus Press anthologies *Local Wonders (ed. Pat Boran)* and *Romance Options (eds. Leeanne Quinn and Joseph Woods), The High Window, The Honest Ulsterman, Ink, Sweat & Tears, The Island Review, Lunate, Neologism, One, Porridge, The Postgrad Journal, The Seamus Heaney New Writing Anthology, The Stony Thursday Book, The Trouvaille Review, The Waxed Lemon* and *The Wild Word.*

My sincere gratitude and appreciation to Amy and Paul for carrying the poetry torch, Craig Jefferson for sharing his creative vision, Derek Yu and From Software for their punishing yet rewarding time sponges, Francis Jones for kind commissions, Jason Lytle for fulfilling a pipe dream, Keith Payne for helpful guidance, Kevin Corstorphine for regularly saying "Hey, dude", Linda McKenna for her encouragement, Matthew and Christine Cordner for never changing, Mel McMahon for continuing friendship and sage editorial precision, MOGWAI for dreamlike soundscapes, Piccola Pizzeria for three decades of culinary quality, Stewart McCullough for putting up with me for a life sentence, the staff in the Ulster Hospital who put me back together again, the Arrell family, the Thompson family and all the loved ones we lost along the way.

I am indebted to the Arts Council of Northern Ireland, whose generous bursary afforded me the luxury of time and space to complete this collection.

Boundless thanks also to Pat Boran, whose words of support and affirmation galvanised the creation of this book.

Above all, I would like to extend my affection to my steadfast Alison (I love you and I like you) and my dear Anna (I could not be more proud of the person that you have become).

Contents

Anticlea / 7

ONE: SEVERANCE
The Slipping Forecast / 13
Errata / 15
Uncoupling / 16
Ascent / 19
Ghost Channels / 20
Adulthood / 21
Menschkeit / 22
Plait / 23
Cut / 24

TWO: DISAPPEARANCE
Midnight in Caravanland / 29
January Violet Blue / 31
The Revenant / 32
Bluebird / 33
Shell / 34
Oymyakon / 35
Words for Snow / 36
A Beach in Fog / 37
Field of Fire / 38
Nightswimming / 39
The Minister's Daughter / 40
Rainbow Lorikeets / 44
Princes Street Gardens, Edinburgh, 2019 / 45

THREE: IMPERMANENCE
Driving in the Dark / 49
Pledged / 50
The Explosions / 51
Hawkhill, Dundee, 1995 / 52
Last Broadcast / 53
Sonnet for a Lost Brother / 54
Sacred Deer / 55
Sisyphus / 56
The Badger / 57

FOUR: CONVALESCENCE
Receiver of Wreck / 61
Harmacy / 62
Falling in the Dark / 64
Intermezzo / 65
On Vulnerability / 67
Stitches / 68
Coming Around / 69
Venipuncture / 70
December / 71
Insomnia Suite / 73
Palinurus / 77

FIVE: ABUNDANCE
Tokens / 81
Resolve / 82
Snacking on Mandarin Oranges
at Patrick Kavanagh's Grave / 83
The Distance / 85
Fireworks Display / 86
Closing Time / 87

for family and friends
thanks to you, the coming dark
is slightly less dark

Anticlea

Afterwards, I ventured beyond the veil,
    the lush meadow where grass-sandalled foothills
parted to bestow a circle of shale,
    the centre of which contained a portal
that echoed with the wails of shades concealed
    deep within the earth: imprisoned phantoms
haunted by past lives in the mourning fields,
    taunted by the lie of pomegranates

and honeyed figs. I journeyed deeper below,
    my mobile phone a lamp to the pathway
of bones, spiderwebs dusting my raincoat
    until the polished throat at last segued
into a wide plateau of asphodel
    and ichor fountains surrounded by crowds
of figures in translucent robes: nobles
    and peasants alike. There, dressed in a shroud

of ivory and narcissi, I spied
    my own mother, wistful and woebegone,
pining for the days before, her doe eyes
    yearning for directions that would not come.
Through a mist of bodies I recognised
    her blurred outline, albeit abraded
by the weight of her premature demise.
    She beckoned. I passed through the ghost parade

and we stood face to glassy face: her gaze
    a thousand leagues away; her silver skin
rippling as if viewed from beneath a lake;
    her voice, once so melodic, now stretched thin.
'Why must you return to this lonely sphere

and linger long after the break of dawn?
Your life is wasting while you idle here.
　　You need to leave, son. It's time to move on.'

One:
Severance

The Slipping Forecast

Viking, North Utsire, South Utsire,
southwesterly 5 or 6 veering northwesterly
4 or 5, backing into East Yamatai.
Moderate or rough, becoming good.

Sweetwater, Trimblefee, Ley Line, Pruck,
magnetic pull veering centrally at first,
heliosphere fragmenting later. Rough or very rough.
Chances of flaming meteors high. Obliteration unlikely.

Nettlesong, Legoland, Linkous, Silverpin,
swathes of fog, white squall, vengeful phantom mariners
returning for stolen gold. Severe gales becoming cyclonic.
Occasionally very violent in Groomsport.

Goldenglove, Solitude, Ghostglow, Trill,
infrequent sightings of city-levelling punch-ups
between Gojira and rival Kaiju, blood-tide tsunamis decreasing 3
at times, Wi-Fi connection erratic, plagues of locusts spotted.

Forties, middle-aged spread sinking southward, inadvertent
afternoon naps increasing, self-loathing 8, weepyclouds 10,
moodswings frequent, anxiety severe, alternating periods of
low and high depression, ennui rough, crises inevitable, staring
nostalgically at childhood drawings of snowmen, every
likelihood of crying over spilt milk.

Tumbledown … Foxwillow … Appleglass … Addlesea …
cosy and carefree middle age spreading to all four corners …

wistful yet blissfully without regret … unhappy but content …
    restful slumber …
not giving two hoots … peace descending

0

to

0.

Errata

This boy at school liked to collect the broken nibs
    of pencils:
dozens of fractured graphite tines he kept inside
    a secret

compartment in a carved wooden case. They rattled
    in his bag
as he walked: a constant reminder of shoddy
    penmanship,

of pressing too hard, holding his Staedtler HB
    at the wrong
angle or clipping tips while gesticulating
    at some fixed

point of interest, squinting while determining
    the distance
of the earth from the sun, wetting his fingerprint
    and tilting

it with a theatrical spin to gauge the course
    of the wind.
I carry my own accidents. The scent of fresh
    sharpenings

and the rattle of breakages, of stick against
    bone, and word
against heart, follows in my wake. We are made of
    these mistakes.

Uncoupling

1. Pared

I loved you, as Damon loved Pythias,
but summer turned cruel when you chose to pull
the pin on our friendship, and years vanished
as if they never happened. Ever the fool,

I mourned after you cut the stem. Grief weighed
heavy as a migraine while you still lived.
Forgive me when I say I felt betrayed,
heart-pained, exchanged like an unwanted gift:

a shaving set, an ill-fitting sweater,
an encyclopaedia of breeds of cat
or last year's calendar. You were never
much of a talker and I liked to chat

too much. I was the irksome splinter
you were just itching to pluck from the tip
of your trigger finger or a winter
cold you blithely shrugged off. You manned the ship

while I gripped the severed anchor, failing
to realise you had already reached
the Fortunate Isles while I was flailing
in the doldrums. There I remained, impeached

for no crime other than being dead weight,
excess cargo that needed to be bucked
overboard while you sailed solo and straight.
Detritus. The grit in oysters you shucked

while hunting for pearls, the acerbic pith
in the orange you peeled from your packed lunch,
the smoking candle when you made your wish
that I would leave. I took the hint, succumbed,

too young to see I had been dumped, forgotten,
too numb to shed any spineless tears
for the lack of things we had in common
apart from the snap of your closing shears.

2. Paired

I loved you like a prisoner loves their captor
the moment before

they shove them into the cellar
and slam shut the trapdoor.

3. Pink Moon

It was only a little lie, white in colour
and soft in texture. It tasted sweet at first,
like fresh peaches or buttercream, when she
invited you for a walk to view the pink moon.

But when you reached for her hand, her fingers
pulled away, the lie turned sour, and the moon
was not really pink at all. It was white, quite white.

4. Pareidolia

Funny how the mind, when still and idle,
drifts on a current of its own design,
returning to the familiar island
you never quite left but instead consigned

to somewhere between Patagonia
and Timbuktu. When you were much younger,
and hoodwinked by love and myopia,
you sought her face in inkblots and summer

clouds, or how a seabird might angle
its wing. Though her eyes appeared clear and kind,
they were merely dewdrops shining on leaves,

or the breeze brushing through tart brambles.
A candle in the dark, the flame twined
around the wick too tight to be uncleaved.

Ascent

i.m.

Following years of taking deadly risks
and defying all the laws of physics,

it was, I regret, inevitable
that when a childhood friend finally fell

like a nest from its cradling parent branch,
this act of momentum would be his last:

gliding downwards past clouds coloured like salt
and the safety of outcrops of flat rock.

So, I invert the image downside up,
and it can no longer hurt quite as much:

his inhaled gasp, the dwindling avalanche
retreating from the point of impact,

his silhouette now suspended in time,
the snow rising through a merciful sky.

Ghost Channels

A small, inky and intense child, he loved to discover
unheard melodies and textures squirrelled in the shadows.

Shying away from a tone-deaf world, he listened closely
for yankee hotel foxtrots ringing through interference,

washing into his inner ear from a nautilus shell:
the marimba of midnight rain on moonsluiced windowsills,

the gated reverb of thunder across wild heather hills,
or the fuzzy felt phantoms that danced in the ant football

between terrestrial channels on a turn-dial TV,
materialising from pixel dots like foo fighters

through feathery cirrostratus clouds or will-o'-the-wisps
in the heart of a deserted wood, visible only

to the eye that pierced electromagnetic, audible
only to the ear still untuned to the rules of the world.

Adulthood

for Dad

Most nights, he calmly crept into my room
    to carefully return the foot that I had poked
from underneath a quilt decorated
    with clockwork robots and shafts of moonlight.

Gently, as if lowering a stretcher
    or defusing a bomb, he eased the limb
back into its womb with a graceful twist.

    Sometimes, just for fun, I feigned sleep and slipped
my heel from its silent orbit to tease
    that hand that swam shark-like with palm
cupped, ready for docking, closing the loop,
    powering down the circuit so I could sleep
soundly, safe in the knowledge that a hand
    would always be there in the dark, guarding.

Menschkeit

for Stewart McCullough

My friend could not help touching the buttons
on a remote control. While watching films,

he absentmindedly brushed his fingers
across the raised grid of coloured rubber

digits – as if strumming an unstrung harp.
All the while, his thumbs trundled on the studs

like a laundry trolley over hotel
carpet or sledge runners on a fresh fall

of snow, the rhythmic duffing like the keys
of a piano stuffed with plump pillows.

Now, when lounging in memory rooms or waiting
in ghostlit hallways, I think of my same friend,

long since left for work in London, and find
myself listening close for the sound of buttons

gently being pressed in the white noise of Lego
settling in its tub, a crow tapping the window

or stiletto heels clipping on chequerboard tiles.
I have tried but have never found the exact sound.

I have not seen him for too long. I miss him.

Plait

Curled up on the kitchen bench, freshly cut
from its parent stem, my daughter's plait
comes alive in a beam of evening light.

The curved tail of a Walt Disney squirrel,
autumnal brown and summer caramel,
at once hardy and vulnerable.

A trio of stands woven together,
unanchored but still flickering, feathered
at the point where scissor blades severed
the flame from the crown of the bonfire
to which it was previously tethered.

Cut

When the power went out with a finger click,
the whole of North Down settled as quiet
as a lake at midnight. Syrupy dim
flooded out of untapped nooks and crannies,
filling rooms from floorboards up with murky
tenebrosity, sending you scrabbling
for candles, oil lanterns and portable
halogen torches: a glowing timeline

of human ingenuity to pacify
your yelping daughter, afraid of the dark
lest it contain snakes or men made of teeth.
Acting the Good Samaritan, you ventured
out to check on friends and elderly neighbours,
braving a street as shadowy and still
as the face of the absent moon, echoes
of distant alarms ringing in filaments

of unlit lampposts, your flashlight a pole star
in your hand. Watching orbs dancing behind
blinds like fireflies in a forest clearing,
you may have thought you heard laughter ringing
in glasses filled with silken wine but then again
you may have willed sound into existence
to prevent the scintillating silence
from reminding you afresh of the time

when, at a tender fifteen, you witnessed
the sudden, fatal accident that sapped
your confidence in where your afterlife
would be spent: you testified at the inquest,
still shaking from the brutal severance

of the fine thread that connects the living
to the dead. It sent you reeling helplessly
like a penny shuffled towards the edge

of a wooden desk. In the mid-90s,
there was no therapy for damaged teens
with PTSD. You woke up screaming
on holiday in Tenerife, haunted
by your own mortality, where your bemused
family procured another Coca-Cola
with no ice – their fear of bacteria
overruled your fear of zombies pulling

you beneath the bed. Ever since your friend
made you watch *The Evil Dead*, that lurid
video nasty of notorious
renown where neither adjective nor noun
suggested puppy dogs and group hugs, you could not
sleep if the landing light was not blaring.
But instead of despairing, you started
preparing in vain for your GCSEs.

Venomous men with black cloaks and bad hair
gave you a hard schooling in spiderwebbed
lairs. Displeased, they seethed at how easily
you excelled at mediocrity, then
handed over your results with a sneer
and a bum steer. Ill-fledged and poorly bred,
you were booted unceremoniously
from the homestead. *The best years of my life,*

my backside, you said, before submerging
those dark thoughts in the same unfathomable
ocean of forgetfulness where you drown
all such emotions. But on sleepless nights

when the sky awaits a blessing of rain
and your ventricles tighten with pain, those same
thoughts float to the surface like burnt logs,
like charred bodies from the belly of the Styx,

like dreams that stream from a prick of morphine
or an acid tab lick with a twist of melon
or a toasted cheddar snack just before
hitting the sack when the ribbon of sleep
is cut with invisible scissors
and the whole shebang goes hammering down
the somnolent turnpike to a labyrinth
of cormorants, jackdaws and cuckooshrikes.

Still, you hold the spark in your fist, the hilt
of a fiery sword that slants the moon
to guide you home in time for the moment
that all of the bulbs in your house stutter
and catch flame. The evening wobbles into
its frame. A radio blares Cyndi Lauper
and is quiet. The freezer fills with frost.

Rooms sleep to dream of what was nearly lost.

Two:
Disappearance

Midnight in Caravanland

When you switched off the television, the sound continued
    to play
like a jazz standard half-remembered, a twinge in the brain,
    a needle in the hay.

You pulled on a jacket, and slipped into a night crackling
    with static
and the promise of rain. The moon was high. Playground
    railings contracted
and creaked as they leaked out the remainder of the day's heat.

The air parted like pashmina as you followed the noise
    of revelry
wafting like a mistral: the magnified whispers and moans
    reverberating

within a dome of cloudless sky. Disembodied voices
    beckoned you
to the promenade: the curved spine of a sleeping giant
    cradling the reflection
of a coruscating universe resting on pin pricks.

Beside the shore, a lone bonfire flickered in the water,
    around which
footloose figures gallivanted, wavering as they slipped
    through each

other, sharing thin strips of glowing embers that they raised
    to hidden lips.
Squinting, you snapped the tableau into focus, then balanced
    the flickering

flame on your fingertip. A magic trick. A geocache
 of image and sound

only you found then gifted back to the trembling darkness
 when you closed your fist.

January Violet Blue

Not blue like a ballroom on an autumn afternoon
    but blue as a bone-cracked saxophone
    still holding the memory of music,
    blue as a flock of blackbirds,
    as a super wolf moon,
    as a crate of empty bottles collecting rain.

Not blue like a snowbound museum bustling with tourists
    but blue as a solitary hay bale
    amassing nests in an unploughed field,
    blue as a bank statement,
    as a withered party balloon,
    as a neglected houseplant weeping leaves.

Not blue like a sea-scored promenade
    but blue as a sewing machine
    corroding at the bottom of a lake,
    blue as a toothless glockenspiel,
    as the cracks in a Chet Baker lullaby,
    as the distance in Betty Draper's eyes.

Not blue like a designer's portfolio
    but blue as a coffee ring
    beside a judgemental coaster,
    blue as an unanswered telephone,
    as an unmanned lost property kiosk,
    as a locked door in a derelict house.

Not blue like a coruscating ceiling
    but blue as a neighbour's security light,
    blaring intermittently
    during the violet blue night
    to notify nobody at all
    of the presence of a passing blue tomcat.

The Revenant

Barefoot on ashlar, I would be at ease
if it were not for the guilt that, sharp as
limoncello, knifes me right in the heart
when I think about how you upped and left
while your loved ones slept in milky June heat,
eluding bailiffs, subpoenas, the pangs
of your conscience ... fleeing to Libertine
City to slake an insatiable
thirst with bottomless dirty martinis,
to guzzle trays of quail eggs and quaaludes,
to frequent all the honky-tonks and howffs
not listed in your dog-eared travel guide.
You nailed each vibrato and arabesque,
sparking off each shady corner, leaving
contrails and constellations of dying
stars in your spangled wake, playing it cool
when police raided the shebeen while a pouch
of joy powder pulsed in your hip pocket.
Breakdown followed breakdown followed breakdown.
An infinite regress of nesting dolls
of the previous selves you had suppressed
with fine white magic and delicacies
finally shook free like neglected teeth.
When the speakeasies ran dry and your friends
amscrayed, you came home, cap in hand, tail tucked
between shaking legs, hoping for a straight
path, an open gate, a loving embrace ...
or you would have done had you not erased
yourself from this portrait. Look: there you are,
dwindling like a bubble in a pipette,
blithely flashing a gap-toothed grin, one hand
extended from an unwashed cuff to touch
life afresh or demand your money back.

Bluebird

for Paul and Amy

Stealing across the edge of town around midnight,
I cleared it all the way home and did not brake once:
no speed bumps, roundabouts, blind corners or red lights,
just a laser-guided straight line to the seafront
from the flyover rendered silk smooth by dropping
the car into neutral and letting inertia
do the hard work, streets and unstirred houses plotting
before me as if I dreamt them – or vice versa.

I became Eugene Cernan and Donald Campbell,
skipping like a stone off the contour of a breath;
Amelia Earhart, weightless as Ariel;
and John Henry, hammering on a twilight crest.

Shell

My sister said
    that if I held
        the dislodged nautilus
            to the side of my head

I would hear the wash
        of a distant ocean
            as if eavesdropping
                on a private conversation.

Although I knew it was not
    really the sea
        but the sound of my own breath
            I listened
                nonetheless.

Once I unlocked that pillbox
    by holding the conch
        to my ear like a receiver
            I became a true believer.

There was no way to stop
    the secrets of remote shores
        roaring forth.

I should have known
    that not every open door
        is an invitation.

Oymyakon

for Nessa O'Mahony

A coldness so cold it brings an amnesia
of heat, where permafrost ballerinas

chime on twilight-blue branches, and wolfdogs
on wood chips respond with a dialogue

of muzzle-chilled whimpers. Since slow winter
snapped our thermometers and spilled silver

into cracked vacuum flasks, we were raptured.
Unfiltered sun reanimated sculptures

of nimbus-ringed saints and cruciform Christ
But, with no one outside to tend the ice,

the statues lost their lustre. Once, tourists
from across Europe rushed to our forests

and thermal springs but our shop, post office,
barroom and school are now shut tight, cautious

of braving the chill breath of Boreas
pricking lips and drying up corneas.

Then cold drew close and temperatures plunged.
I have not spotted my neighbours in months.

Words for Snow

crystal, needle, bullet, column, plane, rime,
spearhead, sector, sheath, polycrystalline,

prism, dendrite, hail, gohei, skeletal,
graupel, seagull, particle, gabriel,

diamonddust, stellar, fern, burst, confetti,
lilyglove, chillykiss, mogul, quinzhee,

onding, ninguid, kriplyana, harebloom,
featherleaf, frostbreath, hootlin, heavenboon,

daintyrain, thistlegift, lighterdown, skift,
winterteeth, pennychime, inchinghome, drift,

whitecloudsong, whimsy, mooncurtain, hatpin,
skydoodle, softloop, brieftreasure, sequin,

almondhope, petal, godpromise, dreampost,
comfort, eveningcrisp, sleepwillow, airghost.

A Beach in Fog

Disconcerting to hear the waves without seeing
 the waves,

suddenly lost behind folds of damp gaberdine,
 the blare

of the lifeguard station's loudhailer instructing
 the brave

seabathers, faintly visible through opaque drapes,
 to come in

to safety but there they doggedly remain,
 bleached sun

shapeshifting their bone-pale shadows into rainbows
 on chrome,

oxidised in mist and synchronised to the swash
 of foam,

suck of undertow, whip of red flags
 and the glare

of sunlight struggling to pierce this glass bowl of fog.

Field of Fire

It had not rained for weeks, and the wheat field
by the dual carriageway was husk-dry, parched,
ready to go up at the slightest spark.

The crops flamed for hours. The blaze would not yield
to the pulsating reservoir relayed
by the fire brigade. The fight was hard won

and when done the land looked scorched by the sun,
sulphur-kissed, battle-scarred, a tacky lake
of spilt tar. The wind smelled sharp as burnt beer.

A steaming haze hung like a startled flock
of birds pinned to the air, an action shot
of a disturbed cloud of dust that, when cleared,

revealed that all the trees survived. No leaf
was scathed and no trunk was charred though the ground
about hissed with residual heat. We found

a miracle just like the untouched fleece.
Sometimes gentle mercies can be observed
in this peculiar, mercurial world.

Nightswimming

A jumble sale of loosened jeans, discarded shirts
and hastily abandoned shoes trails a higgledy
catenary from sandbank to jagged shoreline.

These garments quiver like pennants, ringing
with the voices of friends hopped up on hormones
and adrenalin, sprinting full throttle to an expectant sea.

Beneath the light of a bashful demilune,
the water appears quite black, like blood on snow.
Undeterred, your gang tears a barefoot path to the rim

of a shadowed parabola. When you break through,
as a needle pricks the skin, the shock knocks the air
clean out of your lungs, but in that moment,

when all is muffled, wrapped in cloth, floating between
the seaweed and the stars, you forget about sharks
and shipwrecks lurking beneath your pinwheeling feet.

The Minister's Daughter

She was suddenly projected in the bedroom window
parallel with my own,
pulling the curtains across a backdrop of indie rock
posters and poetry anthologies

that foreshadowed our first conversation: joking about
Morrissey and his penchant
for hearing aids and gladioli. We were teenagers, and while I was all
the things that tender age brings –

awkward, idealistic and maudlin – she was bright as pins
and wore her willowy skin
so confidently she might have been another species.
Our schools were twinned,

and most days we rode the bus together to the outskirts
of the town where we lived,
cul-de-sacs, avenues and lanes stuttering past and through
the frame

as talk small and big flowed with a natural ease I have
rarely felt since.
I was in awe of her intelligence and eloquence
that any fool could clearly see

in spite of her humility, and while it was only
ever platonic
I still felt pangs of curiosity about brushing
the meniscus of her fingertips

or tracing the outline of her Cupid's bow above parted
lips but it would have been uncouth
to take those risks and blame it on the ignorance of youth.
Still, I was aflame

with envy when she stepped out with a childhood friend
who treated her terribly.
I can picture her now, clear as an autumn afternoon,
peering from behind the door,

puffed eyes, flushed cheeks and bow-string quivering.
I was guilty by association
but stronger magnets cannot choose which metals they attract
and which they should repel.

Some nights, I kept watch for when stars transformed into arrows,
their fiery arcs
dancing around the manse, and her light clicked off, and the drapes
went black and still

as an undisturbed lake, taking comfort in the knowledge
that she was safe
and racking up another day of distance from heartbreak,
settling down

under the same covers on which I often sat, tapping
and drumming
as she played and replayed her favourite vinyls
while I wittered on

without a breather (Beastie Boys, Pixies, Weezer),
just happy to be welcomed
within the circle of trust, worthy of her mother's smile
and her father's

grunts of begrudging approval, certain this was a place
where I was not viewed
as a misfit, an oddball or the runt of the litter
unlike the looks

I received from everyone else from the librarian
to the babysitter.
In her clandestine solar system of records and books,
I needed no more proof

of the beautiful but burdensome immortality
of youth.
I should have held on to it for longer. Years passed. We both
moved away. Life happened.

She was destined for an Oxbridge First while I was locked in
on a 'Desmond' –
a 2.2 for those who don't know. I could not hold a candle
to her talent

nor could I prevent a ruthless moon from waxing gibbous
or waning crescent
in a universe indifferent to my lachrymose
and futile laments

to halt time as if threading a button onto a shirt
that no longer fits.
Just last week I found myself driving on that same street.
Our former houses

looked exactly as if the minister's daughter and I
never left:
the same salt-beaten boards and bollards in need of fresh paint,
the same frowning roofs,

the same dejected squares of grass thirsting for blood and bone,
and the same
slipstreams of fibres and light beaten between our front doors,
itching to be

discovered by future sons and daughters in this languid
and lonesome town.

Rainbow Lorikeets

A jaunt to Edinburgh zoo where rows of nesting doll cages glister
    in ailing October sun.

The year spills the last few coins left in her purse to barter for
    more time.
        You pay no mind to the diminishing light.

Like a pro athlete, you outrun your mum, breathless, zeroing in
    on the Bright Birds exhibit depicted

in the folded map you doggedly grip in your gloved fists.
    Within moments,

those hands that look like mine are unsheathed and outstretched,
    quivering inside a miniature aurora borealis

as you lift up tiny nectar cups from which Thumbelina birds
    can sip,
        minuscule wings and beaks purring

as you conduct colour itself, blurred crotchets and quavers
    perched on your fingers
        as you giggle and chirp in harmony.

I remain in awe of your gifts. You are wonderful.
    Precious. You can do anything.

Princes Street Gardens, Edinburgh, 2019

Just before closing time,
    we snuck
        into the sunken park
                where the dark,
                    a special kind of Scottish dark,
                coated trees and grass
            like the water
        that once filled
      this former loch,
and for the briefest
    of moments
        we lost track
            of the hour
                and moved
                    like basking sharks
                between the fibreglass
            shards of Halloween
        cold, the bitter
      scent of spent fireworks,
hops wafting from the brewery
    like the coming snow,
        and the greenery
            that shimmered
                behind the air
                    like anemone and waterwheels,
                and all the while
            the words to express
        how beautiful I found
      this evening,
your mother and you,
    caught in my throat
        so I wrote them down

on borrowed paper
as soon as we returned
to our hotel.

Three:
Impermanence

Driving in the Dark

1.

The landscape stretches deep and dark as the Mariana trench
as we circuit an elliptic peninsula overwatched
by the melanomorph blockade of Magilligan prison.

Another foray into the gloaming after another
unsuccessful attempt to teach you to cross the Rubicon
of sleep, so we resort to the only formula that works:

heat whacked up to sweltering, calming strains of Classic FM
bathing the cabin, you all bumfled up in your romper suit
as the car bullets past hedges and fields, headlights revealing

dashes painted on the road marking out a sedative code
that finally, after significant distance, coaxes you
into a long overdue stupor. Thumb in, eyes closed, tilted

back in your moulded seat, you doze like a champion, the windows
cracked slightly open to let out the subtropical closeness.
We slope home, folding sea to our left, purring grass to our right.

2.

Back at the house, I scoop you up, pressing you gently against
my chest, then lower you into your bunk, taking care to tuck
your stray foot underneath the quilt, then slip out in case you stir

like silt silently rising in a pond. I collapse into
bed at last, exhausted and overwrought, where my mind keeps on
driving for miles in the dark, my body wide awake.

Pledged

Bedtime but abruptly interrupted by the scuff
of a manilla envelope being clumsily shoved
beneath my dormitory door, snagging slightly
on raggedy wood as it shuffles like a hockey

puck across cheap fibrous carpet, dove white
in migrainous strip light, stuffed like a drug
drop, not with crisp fifties but with a sheaf
of neatly folded sheets of lyrics: the entire

discography of a long-since defunct indie
band copied out longhand in Sharpie bold
and bruised as a confession, countless screeds
of lovelorn sentiments burning inkwell fires

on the page, so full of secondhand yearning,
such a plundered bounty of mid-90s ennui
ventriloquised in the rehearsed cursive of a heartsore
introvert whose true identity I never discovered.

The Explosions

When the news broke I desperately tried
to call and text but the network had died

and fallen limp as a snapped angling line.
I grew increasingly panicked each time

it failed to connect, picturing your corpse
entombed within strata of collapsed floors

and choking rush hour dust, hidden within
the skeleton of a sunken building.

Then your message came through. I almost wept.
You were safe, unscathed but were forced to trek

home in thick July heat. With no transport,
the streets in London were hiving with scores

of punch-drunk commuters doing the same,
monogrammed cuffs rolled tight as tourniquets,

ties drooping loose from their designer shirts.
Dazed, as if they had just arrived on Earth.

Hawkhill, Dundee, 1995

On Monday mornings I was awoken
    by the echo of beer kegs thundering
        into the cellar of the pub next door.

It was the sound of shells being loaded
    into a cannon: a guttural roar
        that rattled the windows when each barrel

fracked the earth's core; a salvo of hollow
    galumphs dredging up from the ocean floor
        followed by the inevitable round

of cursing when a runaway firkin
    burst its hoops and staves in a frothy spray
        of rivets and ale. I came to know Graeme

and Jan by name: their Dundonian brogue
    cut through cigarette smoke and my window
        in the flat on the backbone of the town

built up around an extinct volcano.
    While the men worked like Trojans I remained
        bundled in eiderdown, dormant until

disturbed around twilight, shaken awake
    by creatures rooting loudly in the bins
        in the alley. Peeking between the blinds,

I caught an urban fox, its entire frame
    a fiery salute, its defiant snout
        testing the air for predators or prey.

Last Broadcast

i.m. Stephen Thompson

1.

He knew just how to work a radio,
    how to strip thin tips from taut magnet wire
then fix them to each end of the diode,
    methodical, as if stringing a lyre.

Like setting a broken bone, he mounted
    the contraption on the board, then fine-tuned
analogue pots and knobs, still astounded
    by his own alchemy when voices crooned

through frequencies. A disciple catching fish,
    he reeled in signals before they could fade,
navigating channels, sweeping bandwidth
    for quadrophonic songs, forecasts and plays.

2.

Some time later, he turned down the silence
    while lying on a hospital gurney,
in awe of the spiked, algae-green skyline
    of his cardiogram and its journey

into oily water: a one-way flight
    to the other side where no theremin,
antenna or Ouija board amplified
    his voice after static had entered in.

Sonnet for a Lost Brother

Relatives remark I am just like him.
The same awkwardness, the same doom and gloom,
the same dark humour and lopsided grin.
We both found corners in circular rooms.

De facto only child without a twin,
I longed to put on my childhood costume.
We were pachinko balls avoiding pins
descending towards a lone wolf blood moon.

Today, I ride this painful carousel,
his ghost astride the stallion to my right,
the remnant of a dislocated arm

with no joint to be dislocated from.
I cast a shadow because of his light.
I touch the heavens because he first fell.

Sacred Deer

A wave of my hand … then the streaming platform buffers
and conjures phantoms on the screen: two louche aristocrats

kitted out in finest Harris tweed for an afternoon
of tracking red deer in the stern glare of a frigid sun.

With matching quilted gilets flecked by whin and clay, they keep
warm with laddish banter and nips from a custom hip flask

of single malt the cost of a sports car. They laugh it off,
and libate a few drops in honour of the stag they will

soon kill, their rifles cocked in unison at the promise
of fresh venison, then continue laughing when they fell

a young buck, its flank full of shot, its splendid form crumpled
in thick gorse barely disturbed by an ill wind, their mouths wide

open as they daub ruddy cheeks with blood as if weeping,
rendered immortal by unfettered red swathes and the feast

in which they will partake before the credits roll and they are
sucked back through the portal, genies into their respective

bottles, their avatars digitally preserved in spite
of the fact that their real-life counterparts since lost the fight:

fallen in the field, their ichor spilt, their miasma gone
into ground and grass where the stag lies with leaves in its maw.

Sisyphus

Still, the rain batters Bangor Blues, spatters
the back yard. A Belfast sink, excavated
from the soil like a wisdom tooth and used
now as a planter, is overflowing,
sluicing out slices of chipped crockery
buried for drainage: a tip gleaned from years
of absorbing *Gardeners' Question Time.*

Strange how these things lodge in the brain
like the stray leaves that stubbornly clog
the unmaintained gutters and drains.

Over by the barren apple tree, branches
long since gone the way of the open fire,
a sweaty polytunnel is flagging,
sagging beneath the cumulated weight
of a standard Northern Irish summer.

But inside the fruit is dry, safe and warm …
and so are we. Grateful now for secure
walls, however stained, a garden facing
south that emblazons with ghost branches
and burning blades late in the afternoon,
for a soft apple bed and a kitchen
that smells faintly of buttered toast.

We are blessed. We have more than most.

The Badger

for Mark Roper

Locked down for weekless weeks, I could not sleep.
Fatigued by a chronic lack of fatigue,
I stumbled through moonfeathered streets

that could have been dreamt into existence:
caramel lamplight, card-ruffling privet
and red-brick walls shimmering, as if wet,

heavy with summer, still warm to the touch.
I ambled to Ward Park where swans and ducks
were roosting, burbling softly on the cusp

of the pond in which a lissom heron
stood proud beneath an ellipse of urban
barbastelles. He sensed me, then abandoned

his kingdom, swimming up into the sky.
I surveyed the realm that was now mine
when a flash of white on black caught my eye:

a coarse humbug, a rotund *Othello*
tile, announced himself with arpeggios
and porcine snorts from nearby undergrowth.

He bolted forth from bushes, unclipped claws
skittering on loose gravel, snout and jaws
steaming like a ready kettle, paunch taut

with fear and fury, chassis thick with earth
and twiggy musk. I had invaded his turf.
He challenged me, all puffed up with fur and girth,

nubby ears pricked like miniature kites,
no doubt the same chancer who a few nights
before ransacked my flowerbeds, go-faster stripes

stained by bruised hibiscus and rose petals,
his pelt dotted with smudged pollen, saddle
and rump still ferrying clumps of speckled

delphinium. I might have thought he grinned
if his wiry hackles were not raised like pins
to a magnet. I flinched then saw him spin

and sprint back to his sett, his stubby tail
ruddering as he raced off to regale
his clan with the tale of a domestic male

who bore the pungent scent of printer ink
and Blue Mountain shampoo, and who dared slink
unprepared into his patch on the brink

of a nervous breakdown. Meanwhile, I sloped
home to a house filled with the comatose
sighs of my safely slumbering family. Alone

again, face to face with my mirror-fetch,
I inspected my reflection for evidence
of a unchecked desire to retrace my steps

and rejoin my nocturnal, feral brethren.

Four:
Convalescence

Receiver of Wreck

It takes its toll, you know, when you collect
so many bruised apples and broken parts,
when the sea concedes so much submerged wreck

into your hands and expects that your heart
will not weigh heavy from such a levy,
from the pricking of all these poison darts,

from the fostering of unsteady
fledglings, from stitching and tending their wounds
before letting them fly free, when ready.

Harmacy

Something has dislodged inside my dad's chest,
rattling as he labours to catch his breath.
A burr reverberates behind his ribs:
a loose rivet clattering, an unfixed

cog in a faulty watch that loses time
while we drive to fetch bromelain and dried
ginger, anything to ward off the cough
settling in his lungs like a choking fog.

He barks and croaks as I move up the gears,
discomfited by the thought he might tear
the lining in his windpipe or, Heaven
forbid, crack a rib. There is no telling

him. He sulks as we coast from hill to hill,
point blank refusing the need for pills
while he restrains the urge to wheeze and rasp,
his diaphragm bristling with fibreglass.

Revenants of past lives add to my fears:
the wraiths of asbestosis from his years
in the shipyard, inhaling secondhand
smoke in common rooms or scaling unmanned

chimney stacks that the bravest steeplejacks
refused to climb. As he blusters and hacks
into a handkerchief, his body quails
like a steam engine coming off the rails

but with watery eyes and shallow voice
he argues tooth and nail about my choice

to escort him to the shopping centre
to request medicine for his tremors.

At the pharmacy, he strunts in an aisle
lined with shelves of nostrums, tinctures and vials
of knock-off perfume until I frogmarch
him like a child to a counter pockmarked

by years of sovereigns and biro tips.
I buy a raft of antibiotics
from a chemist resembling a pencil
if it spoke and wore horn-rimmed spectacles.

Back in the car, Dad guzzles a handful
from the box washed down with several gulps
of cold coffee. 'Shake me and I'll rattle,'
he mumbles through a mouth stuffed with marbles.

'Strong as an ox,' he says but continues
to cough. Every vessel and sinew
within his tired frame rumbles like pebbles
tumbling inside a barrel. The perils

of the modern age could not faze a man
raised between the wars, and who saw firsthand
air raid shelters, rationing, polio …
so what would his mollycoddled son know

about the price of fish? I hold my whisht
while he shifts his weight in his seat, the swish
of blazer beneath seatbelt the lone sound
aside from the ostinato of ground

under rolling wheels, the car a stylus
dropped in a groove that plays only silence.

Falling in the Dark

Not my finest moment, I have to say:
misjudging the number of stairs to go tumbling
downwards as if into a dunking pond,

to feel the floor beneath my feet give way, suddenly,
before dropping swiftly like a faulty lift,
soundtracked by the snare drum crack of my left

ulna snapping like kindling, the cymbal
crash of a rash of curses as my wrist
locked into a mechanism on the fritz

with molten hot rods and springrazor cogs,
the same gammy arm I broke as a child
that never healed quite straight, and rightly nixed

my ability to play power chords, perform
conjuring tricks or embrace my girlfriend
without hearing my joints click, a lifetime

of calamity that has since cast me
adrift on a sinister sea of codeine
and troubled daydreaming, with frequent trips

to the moon from which vantage point the world
below appears dim and slow yet the echo
of breaking my feeble bones still makes me wince.

I fell as a child and have been falling ever since.

Intermezzo

And the reason that I fell?

Embarrassed to admit
   that I banjaxed
      forearm, elbow and wrist
         while conducting my nightly rounds:

checking the perimeter
   for weaknesses,
      ticking off the to-do list
         of windows and locks
            to keep out the wolf and fox,

child soundly asleep in her cot,
   wallet safe at all costs,
      dog ensconced in her crate,
         deadbolt pulled on the side gate
            to prevent it from banging,
               no sign of tarantulas,
                  scorpions or snakes.

An inventory
   I work through methodically
      to stop my brain from clanging
         like a storm drain
            after a heavy fall of rain.

And then, typically inept,
   I misjudged the distance between the steps
      and the ground

– I try not to think
   of that ungodly sound
      but my mind insists –

and wrenched the bone's distal third
   so hard it smarted like an asterisk.

On Vulnerability

The surgeon plays me like an instrument,
tapping a tune around my clavicle
as if divining the exact spot to extract
watery sap from a cactus, a self-defence

death grip that leads her to burrow deep between
shoulder bones, seeking out a tree knot
filled with medals, antique coins or, if I must
explain, pain. 'There, yes, that's us just there,'

she says, and the nurse, amenable as rain,
injects me with a 'swift gin and tonic'
that straightaway causes my left arm to start
sleeping on the job, docile as a lapdog

without either a bite or a bark,
the first of my parts to shut down and go dark.
It's pathetic, really, how petrified I am
that I might not wake from the anaesthetic,

that my heart might stop, that I might remain
locked in blankety limbo, and how, as fog
rolls in, as time bends and shrinks, my mind scrabbles
to think of metaphors and rhymes to describe

this heightened awareness of being alive,
to defer the primal fear that when the light
grows dim, the knives are all stored away and the line
goes slack, no one will remember to reel me back.

Stitches

try not to think about the blade ringing
before it unseams pink and pregnable flesh

like a holdall being forced open at customs
to be checked for counterfeit goods

zipper teeth clacking as they separate
to reveal your earthly possessions

the burgundy and ivory lining
of the inner canvas
rippling slightly in sterile air

with nothing to declare
but your weakness

Coming Around

Following surgery, I sleep for three days,
occasionally surfacing from a haze
of quicklime and blue lotus when a nurse daubs
iodine and dried blood from skin around gauze
and plaster while another runs from pillar
to post to fetch me ice chips and painkillers,
my own arm still running down the clock
of the effects of a hefty dose of nerve block.

When I move, my phantom limb lollops by my side,
trailing behind like an ungainly child,
a disobedient chunk of uncarved lumber,
a telephone with no connecting number,
puppeteered by heart monitor and cannula,
the xylophone of sutures that ladder the entire
length chiming within the fog like a blind choir.

Doctor McCocksure hmmms at the manual
clipped to the foot of my adjustable bed, then scrawls
gibberish in liquorice ink while the wall
behind his hundred quid haircut warps and blurs.

I am grateful for small blessings. I am alive,
well and warm. People starve. It is snowing outside.

Venipuncture

After several unsuccessful attempts
to siphon a fresh sample of my lifeblood,

the kindly nurse gives it up as a bad job
before I become pincushioned, cross-stitched,

my elbow crook a wonky constellation
of weeping dots floating in a murky

purple cosmos bursting towards my wrist.
'Looks like you truly are your mother's son,'

she mutters after I slur that I have veins
just like my mum: gossamer thin, these nervous

wires stubbornly refuse to be pierced, curving
away from the syringe like fishing lines

slipping off the hook, leaving lily pads
of burst capillaries blooming on the surface.

December

for Keith Payne

Liberated at last, you are wheeled to a foyer fragranced with
apples and samphire, a brown paper bag containing a pick and
mix of painkillers nestled in your lap, and not for the first time
you feel like a hobo boozing on a Baltimore street corner.

Beneath a sickly exit sign, sliding doors repeatedly tear a gap in
the penumbra, revealing an obscene ensemble of smokers
huddling around a shared lighter, their shaggy merged outline
bristling through a melange of nicotine and doleful sleet.

A disembodied Michael Bublé, the Ghost of Christmas Jazz,
gives it laldy from the heavens while the canteen of cutlery
freshly bolted into your flimsy ulna contracts in the cold (the
following summer, you will attempt to go wild swimming at
Dunseverick and last a feeble five minutes) as you wait for your
wife to collect you.

It could have been worse, of course. Much worse. An itinerary
of casualties plays in your mind like the IN MEMORIAM
section at the Oscars: your neighbour who, after nodding off at
the wheel, drove his Honda Civic off the carriageway and
dusted pelvis, sternum and both arms beyond repair; your
brother who, while taking photos of a marching band, slipped
on a mossy wall and impaled himself on a railing so deeply
in his oxter that paramedics were forced to fetch an angle
grinder to trim the malevolent arrowhead; and the town drunk
who, while doddering to the tumbledown farm where he lived
via an unlit backroad, was clipped by a van and pirouetted
breathlessly towards Cassiopeia.

Snap! and you're back in the room – or more accurately, the multi-storey car park built like a brutalist icebox. Your breath beads against your unkempt beard. It takes you three cack-handed attempts to coax the seatbelt across a limb cocooned in plaster decorated with reindeer and snowmen. It finally clunk-clicks. As the car maunders through the fuzzbox countryside, the dark welcomes you like an honoured guest. Flakes burst against the windscreen like fat, somnolent moths – a fireworks display for a fun-sized village. Admittedly, there are more unpleasant ways to spend an evening. Gratitude is a choice.

Insomnia Suite

1. More Weight

There are days when you can react to the detractors
like Giles Corey in the apocryphal story:
defying the Puritans to load on another stone.

It's really no bother. Your ribs and shoulders
can withstand the pressure of the heaviest boulders.
Your skin can repel the fiery slings and quills
of a hundred cawing crows and their ill wills.

On other days, however, your thread could be severed
by a blade as sharp as a chaffinch feather.
A kick from a kitten's paw could knock you over.

Hard to predict exactly how each day will feel
when your spirit tips like a seesaw and spins like a wheel.

2. Phantom

for Kevin Corstorphine

Strange sounds hovered like mist on the surface
of the estuary, dusting the night
with high notes on the rim of a wineglass.

Locals said that with the right wind you might
hear something like a child crying, something
like an ancient culling song, and something

like a bird and yet nothing like a bird.

3. Impatient

hospital time crawls
like ghost clocks in casinos:
slow and slower still

4. Lying in the Dark

5 in the AM. It has been chucking
it down for hours: a ruckus of rainfall
that transcends pitter-pattering showers,
bucketing onto patios, gutters,

fences and garden sheds. The unrestrained
force of it has plucked you from the routine
of a world quite rightly tucked up in bed
and dunked you in this planetary snafu:

a lonely galaxy where rest remains far, far,
away along with the chance to place blame
because whose fault is it when the rain
becomes more of an assault than a serenade?

5. Sea Frets

At night, when sleep refuses to arrive
    like the sea stubbornly avoiding the shore,
        worry returns as a burglar tests for unlocked doors.

I find myself perusing a mental shelf
    of my most shameful blunders and heinous lies,
        each one well-thumbed and Dewey Decimal Classified,

some rubbed smooth as tanners from being turned
      over like soil. I hope for pure gold but dredge up crude oil,
            black as burnt apples and sour as dried blood. A flood

of the stuff gushes forth from the bluff,
      too powerful to be silenced or snuffed. When sleep
            finally descends, it comes with a noose and a gun.

6. Morning Valediction

Rain, like sadness, tapping insistently
      on a wavering rectangle of glass,
            wakes you from an already unsettled

sleep: a brain on high alert, a bone ache
      that no number of painkillers could dull,
            and a mattress that fails to tame

your wild conniptions ... stumbling into pale
      blue stillness of zero dark, the domain
            of cats and insomniacs, you might think:

this is why people drink ... a restless bed
      pushes folk over the edge. This is why
            people lose the will. This is why they kill.

7. A Caravan in the Rain

   for Matthew Cordner

How delicious to fade away to the pachinko melody
      of rain
that wipes clean the scoreboard and erases the day's zero sum game,
      a migraine

lifting,
a heatwave
giving way
so we can slip into the snowy centre of a ball of wool
and filtrate
our corporeal weight through the drumming of hundreds of digits,
these waves
of fluid paradiddles that invite us - warm, safe, unanchored –
to break
through the confines of this cruel and unsparing cosmos …
to let go of the reins.

8. A Notion

for Mel McMahon

It begins with a tingling: the slightest
tug of a fish on the line or a kite
in the wind, like meeting someone you might
know in the street and reaching for that name

that does not come but taunts you from the tip
of the tongue like a gargoyle warding off
this temporary state of being numb.
You might feel it spreading beneath your limbs:

a cushion of damp sand that releases
the rowboat leeward, straying far from shore,
balefire and mooring until it idles
to the heart of blank slate lake, where its keel

relays a series of waves that instructs
your mind, straggling behind in the shallows,
to swim to the deep, to join the body
in this blissful reprieve of healing sleep.

Palinurus

A blister pack branded ZOLPIDEM, embossed majuscule
raised like braille or gooseflesh, slips into my trembling palm.

I intend to pop one before schlepping to bed before sinking
into the River Lethe, hoping that a monkey's paw side effect
switcheroo will not cause me to oversleep like Aurora or Ash
until after the bombs have dropped and my hometown is razed
to its founds. Disdaining fortune, I chase the blue pill
with a round of toasted wheaten and a tumbler of warm milk.

In a spell I am punch-drunk, dishevelled in the bathroom,
teeth singing a demented shanty in sync with my brushing
before I am shoved overboard by traitorous hands, plunging
past angler fish and bathyspheres, past coral and bladderwrack
towards a luminescent biome of cobalt and indigo.

Spark out, I drift through shoals of spiny lobster and langoustine
until the water thickens with amniotic syrup, black rift expanding
in all dimensions as I flop like a Maine Coon on the lap of oblivion.

If I wake, I will be on a distant shore, naked aside
from a loincloth of dulse and damp sand, discombobulated,
combing through a month's worth of beard for stray urchins,
hunting in vain for the shyster who left me so draggle-tailed.

Five:
Abundance

Tokens

At the youth fellowship Christmas party,
my dad, in his footloose prime and giddy

with postwar energy, wins a bumper
bar of chocolate, its regal wrapper

bearing a cursive script reserved for cards
from the Palace. Considering this hard

slab of contraband swaddled in embossed
foil, he pays no mind to either the cost

of the precious ration or his sweet tooth,
choosing instead to offer it as proof

of his true affection to the comely
girl across the aisle, holding this relay

baton with a hand scarred by the shipyard
but confident, inviting her towards

a life together and this simple twist:
without chocolate I would not exist.

Resolve

So many years wasted on hammering myself
into a round hole
and squeezing my star into a square mould,

of doing my damnedest to follow codes
and social cues
to pretend my bright colours do not bleed

over the lines, that my blood does not smudge
the shade
of a beta reject on litmus tests

for the alpha male brigade: so much time
misspent
chasing after a self-creation myth

and the white whale of straight A grades to please
sociopaths
who write the rules of a meet-cute crapshoot

I could never win with a broken brain
and abnormal skin.
So, I accepted weekly prescriptions

of caustic judgement and buried them deep
within
where they took root like mare's tail and affixed

like bindweed, restricting my perception
of my own worth
instead of recognising that frailty

and inner strength are often the same thing.

Snacking on Mandarin Oranges
at Patrick Kavanagh's Grave

A dreich January afternoon finds us slowly winding around
    Inniskeen,
drapes of winter rain parting as we cross deep-rooted borders
    of both history

and time, trespassing on estates as decades flutter past windows
    slick with rivulets
that distort the indistinct shapes outside, the strata of terrain
    and souterrain

rumbling beneath and all around the car, the wipers repeatedly
    revealing
then obscuring shivering trees and sheets of petroglyphs
    hidden inside the steam.

We idle aimlessly with no end point and no coordinates,
    dislocating
from grinding routines and expectations, hemmed in only
    by bristling hedges,

not caring how we arrive wherever we are going or not going until,
pilgrimage fulfilled, we get to the site where the air is more dry
    but no less chill.

A gentle stroll from parked car to graveyard brings us to the
    hallowed spot where untold
wayfarers have paused to take a moment, shoot the breeze,
    smoke a sneaky cigarette

and reflect on the brevity of this gift called life, the poetry concealed between
sheathes of wheat or stashed inside knots of trees, boots rooted in the same gravel

displaced by the giants and pioneers who came before us. The heft of it is enough
to shorten the breath, but just before there is no air left you happen to conjure

a clutch of oranges from your jacket, each one pocked like a miniature planet
plucked from its orbit, each bright as holy flame, dispelling the greyness of the season.

The Distance

for Anna

In the dream you are tearing up the beach
    at full steam, scampering hell for leather
        towards some magical spot that has caught

your eye. You have forgotten your parents
    and the leash you were in charge of holding.
        The dog, emboldened by newfound freedom,

tries to bolt but I grab hold of her nape
    before she can escape. You, however,
        have become a sun-blurred whirr of motion,

rattling pell-mell, your outline turned golden
    and fuzzy, indistinct. I foolishly
        think that you will soon turn and wave and shout,

'Daddy, keep up!' but your legs have become
    a pinwheel of bare skin, your arms churning,
        your determined fists punching through air, clouds

and the stratosphere towards Rainbow Road,
    Columbia, Endor and Solitude.
        The universe is yours to grab and hold
with both hands. Never come back down to land.

Fireworks Display

A benign kind of lunacy: this throng
of people assembled in the darkness,
waiting for the show to start, a few wrong
steps from jagged rocks and the suck and wash

of a shoreline fissling like sweet wrappers
in the previews before a matinee.
A *whoosh*. The sloped roof fills with firecrackers,
pistils and flying fish: a sensory

overload of weeping willows, crossettes
and fountains puncture clouds black as cola;
the ecstatic truth of watching comets,
liquid fire and blooming girandola

as if witnessing the birth of our earth;
the full extended repertoire of stars
and planets captured in microfiched bursts
of memory to be replayed in hard

winter months as proof that the charred remains
of summer can be reignited when
we find ourselves repeating this refrain:
the finale is not always the end.

Closing Time

for Pat Boran

Who does not love this ritual of drawing curtains:
this simple gift that heralds the day's end of play,
that drives away the wolf and sends the painbirds
back to their nest. How the ear tingles as gliders
tut contentedly like beads on an abacus, counting

off seconds with easing breaths, shutting up shop
to the clamour of frantic static that hammers at
the base of the skull: that damned persistent
migraine that rolls back and forth like a boulder
across the floor of the brain; the fog that comes

with the drudgery of unfolding a roadmap while
wearing oven gloves. But how streets and traffic
recede from view with the tug of a blind and the flick
of a switch. The lighting of lamps is akin to taking
well-thumbed books down from a shelf: the perfect

timing of descending the stairs just as the central
heating fills up the ground floor like a warm bath.
Give the switchboard a rest: the data stream can
buffer and crash; tomorrow's portion of sorrow can
be cached until this night has paid the tax of sleep.

· · ·

...

(hidden track

and here,
the needle
dunts the run-off groove …

the music stopped
while you were
nodding off,

and that
bumping sound,
that soft-cushioned heartbeat,
is a rowboat nudging

a distant jetty at
the archipelago
of the lands between:

Amity,
Rapture,
Koholint
and Zihuatanejo …

a chance to slip
into nothingness,
throw

away the oars,
fade to black,
scroll back
to the cold open,

and start over, start over, start over …)